W9-BSC-531

WESTMONT JR. HIGH SCHOOL

DIST.
6665   591 LEE
working with animals

WORKING WITH

ANIMALS

exploring
careers

WORKING WITH

ANIMALS

By Barbara Lee
Introduction by Barbara Sher

Westmont Jr. High School
Media Center
Westmont, Illinois 60559

Lerner Publications Company • Minneapolis

For Ben, Molly, and Timothy

Acknowledgments

My thanks to the dozen people profiled in
this book, who freely gave me hours of their
time. And thanks also to the many friends
and strangers—too many to name here—
who helped me find just the right people
to interview.

The Exploring Careers series was developed
by Barbara Lee.

Copyright © 1996 by Barbara Lee

All rights reserved. International copyright secured. No part of this
book may be reproduced or transmitted in any form or by any
means, electronic or mechanical, including photocopying and
recording, or by any information retrieval system, without
permission in writing from Lerner Publications Company, except for
the inclusion of brief quotations in an acknowledged review.

Library of Congress Cataloging-in-Publication Data

Lee, Barbara, 1945–
    Working with Animals / by Barbara Lee ; introduction
by Barbara Sher.
    p.   cm. — (Exploring careers)
    Includes index.
    Summary: Profiles of twelve people whose diverse careers
involve animals: fish biologist, animal behaviorist, veterinarian,
wildlife manager, zoo educator, animal shelter supervisor, dairy
farmer, wildlife photographer, veterinary technician, jockey, pet
sitter, aquaculturist.
    ISBN 0-8225-1759-0 (alk. paper)
    1. Animal specialists—Vocational guidance—Juvenile literature.
2. Animal specialists—Biography—Juvenile literature. [1. Animal
specialists—Vocational guidance. 2. Occupations. 3. Vocational
guidance.] I. Title. II. Series:
    Exploring careers (Minneapolis, Minn.)
SF80.L43 1996
591'.023—dc20   95-25657

Manufactured in the United States of America
1 2 3 4 5 6 – JR – 01 00 99 98 97 96

CONTENTS

INTRODUCTION

by Barbara Sher

Welcome to the world of work. It's a remarkable world, filled with opportunities, almost too big to understand. There are indoor jobs and outdoor jobs. There are jobs that involve other people and jobs that don't. There are jobs you've never heard of and jobs with names you can't pronounce. And to complicate matters even more, the jobs of tomorrow may not be the same as the jobs of today.

But some things will remain the same. In fact, let me tell you a secret. For successful people, work is like play. That's right—play. That's because they've found the work that is best suited to who they are. Their careers fit their unique talents, their interests, and their skills and education.

Introduction

Begin by asking yourself what you love doing. What is fun? What makes you excited? The answers will give you some clues about what kind of work you might enjoy—and be good at. It's not too early to begin exploring. Talk to your teachers and parents, your friends and neighbors. Ask them to introduce you to people doing work that you would

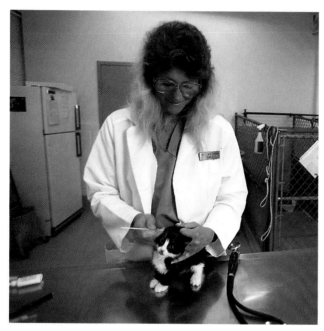

like to find out more about. You will be surprised by how willing people are to talk about what they do. Perhaps they will even show you around their workplaces.

Reading this book is a great start. Without leaving your chair, you will go to work with people who will tell you about what they do and why they do it. They will give you ideas. Maybe their jobs will seem boring or hard. Or maybe they'll excite you. It doesn't matter. It's all part of exploring.

So let yourself be curious. Be a detective. Remember, you don't have to make up your mind right now. You are just collecting information. Good luck. And have fun!

Twelve Careers Working with Animals

We share the earth with many creatures, from the family dog sleeping on the sofa to the billions of insects we hardly think about except when one bites us. We use—and sometimes misuse—animals for food, clothing, transportation, companionship, and recreation. When wild animals are in danger of becoming extinct, we may pass laws to protect them. We build zoos and aquariums to provide homes for animals. Sometimes we put them to work as our eyes and our ears. Our relationships with animals can be deep and emotional.

There are dozens of ways to work with animals, both domestic and wild. Some jobs are traditional and others are more unusual. This book is a behind-the-scenes tour of some of the many careers open to people interested in working with animals.

Twelve Careers

In the pages that follow, 12 people take you into their workaday worlds. Their stories will give you an idea of the skills you need to become a dog trainer or a fish farmer, a fish biologist or a wildlife photographer. Some of these people have advanced college degrees, but many learned on the job. A few people knew from an early age what they wanted to do, while others developed their interests over time. Some people are on the cutting edge of technology. Others do things the old-fashioned way. Each person is different, and each career is different.

If you think that a veterinary technician has nothing in common with a wildlife manager, think again. Although these 12 people have diverse backgrounds and interests, they have more in common than you might expect. Each person worked hard, learned skills, and developed a knack for what they do. If the perfect job didn't come along at first, they learned new skills or volunteered their time until they got the job they wanted.

Each of these 12 people will tell you what they like and don't like about what they do. They have practical tips and suggestions to help you explore a career working with animals. Although these people all work in the mid-Atlantic region of the United States, you can find

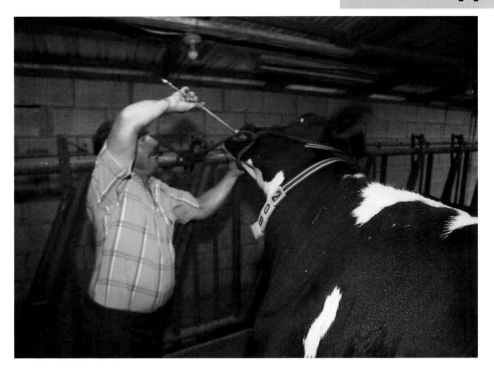

similar jobs in many places. And although no one can predict the future, the people profiled in this book have opinions about how their jobs or professions will change in the 21st century.

Twelve people. Twelve careers. Their stories may surprise you.

Steve Wilson is a dairy farmer, one of many jobs—from the traditional to the cutting edge—that involve animals.

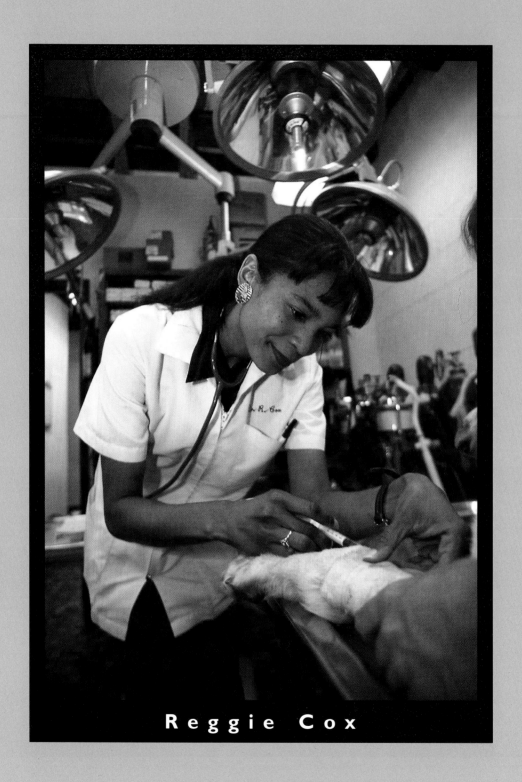

Reggie Cox

Chapter One

VETERINARIAN

When she was three years old, Reggie Cox told her mother that she planned to become a veterinarian. "I don't know why I wanted to do it," she says. "I didn't even know a veterinarian." That didn't stop Reggie. After high school, she completed a degree in biology at the Tuskegee Institute in Alabama and a doctor of veterinary medicine (DVM) degree at the University of Missouri Veterinary School.

She also had plenty of practical experience. As a volunteer at the Jackson Zoo in Mississippi during high school, she learned to treat small animals and birds and conduct laboratory tests in the zoo's hospital. Later, during college, she spent a summer at the National Institutes of Health near Washington, D.C., helping a medical researcher conduct studies on bacteria. Reggie also worked for a veterinarian during college. She dispensed medicines, cleaned the clinic, and assisted in surgery. "It was on-the-job training," she says. Later, as part of her veterinary degree program, she worked in veterinary clinics in Mississippi, Ohio, and New Mexico.

Reggie Cox

But becoming a veterinarian is not the whole of Reggie's story. She also knew from an early age that she wanted to write. "So I made a decision to become a veterinarian and a writer on the side," she says. She is currently writing a book to help children learn to take better care of their pets. She hopes eventually to write a newspaper column about animals.

A Typical Work Week

Reggie works four days a week and every other Saturday in a large veterinary hospital. She is on call every sixth weekend and one weekday evening for emergencies and walk-in patients. One full day each week, she does

> # A lot of different personalities do well with this career.

surgeries. One of the most common operations is spaying and neutering animals to prevent them from having puppies and kittens. Other days, she checks pets for parasites, vaccinates them against rabies and other diseases, and educates owners about their pets' health. These routine appointments make up the largest part of her day. A veterinarian in a smaller practice might have appointments in the morning and perform surgery in the afternoon.

Although Reggie is on call one evening a week, she no longer has to respond to emergencies in the middle of the night. "We now refer patients to an emergency animal hospital after midnight," she says with relief.

Larger hospitals that employ several veterinarians are the wave of the future, because more doctors can share the business expenses and clients. "And I can talk with the other veterinarians about my patients to make sure that I haven't missed something," she says. In unusual cases, such as rare diseases, she contacts specialists or college professors for help.

Patience and Compassion

"A lot of different personalities do well with this career," Reggie says. "I've always been reserved. But I've become more outgoing in order to communicate with owners." A veterinarian needs patience to work with animals. "You get a whole lot further with patience," she says, noting that she's never been bitten. She also believes veterinarians must be compassionate. "Owners are concerned and have a lot of questions, and they need a lot of reassuring."

Reggie also must euthanize, or humanely kill, sick or elderly pets. "It's hard, but by the time the animal is dying, the owners have resolved things in their minds," she says. "So they are usually okay with the decision. Owners don't want their animals in pain." Reggie notes that owners may want her to make the decision, something she doesn't feel she can do for anyone else.

Veterinary School

It's not enough to be patient, kind, and friendly. A vet has to withstand the demands of a four-year college education followed by four years of veterinary school. "It's intensive and a lot of information is presented in a short period of time," Reggie says. In high school, she studied biology, chemistry, algebra, calculus, and physics. At Tuskegee, she completed her biology degree in three years rather than the usual four. She also took courses in chemistry and math. Her vet school program consisted of two years of classroom study, followed by two years of combined academic and clinical (practical)

Reggie's work requires patience with her animal patients and their owners.

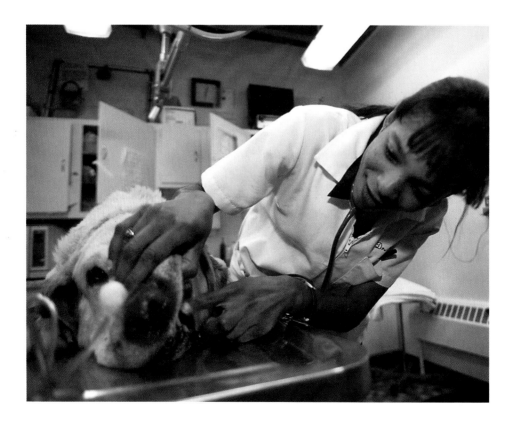

Veterinary Medicine

Veterinarians specialize in treating either large or small animals. Most vets work for animal hospitals that treat small animals such as cats and dogs. Others work with livestock or large animals, often making house calls to farms and ranches. Veterinarians might specialize in treating birds, reptiles, marine (ocean) animals, and wild animals of all species. The work may differ in certain geographical areas. In the Southwest, for example, veterinarians treat exotic animals such as snakes and lizards. Zoos, aquariums, research laboratories, wildlife preserves, and agricultural programs in universities also employ veterinarians.

experience. Reggie believes physical and mental skills are both essential for a veterinarian.

"You need motor (physical movement) skills because you do surgery," she says, "and mental skills because you have to be able to think. You have to ask the owner what the animal was doing. Then you must think what this might mean."

Veterinarians also interpret lab results to do a diagnosis—that is, to identify the disease or problem. "Your diagnostic skills get better over time," she says. For Reggie, working with her animal patients, not their owners, is the most satisfying part of her job.

Reggie examines an X ray of a dog.

A Long Road

Getting into veterinary school can be difficult. In addition to good grades, you must have practical experience working for a veterinarian or at a zoo. "Veterinary schools will not admit you without experience," Reggie says.

Before you can practice as a veterinarian, you must take many exams, starting with a national written exam. It tests a student's knowledge of all aspects of veterinary medicine, from animal biology and diseases to treatments and medications. Reggie took her national exam before she graduated from vet school. She was nervous, she says, but she passed the test on the first try. (Some people take the test several times before they pass.)

Since each state has its own licensing requirements for veterinarians, Reggie took exams for licenses in Florida, Maryland, Mississippi, Kentucky, and Georgia, states where she thought she might like to practice. After graduation, she came to the Washington, D.C., area and accepted a job at the hospital where she still works.

But Reggie isn't through with education. All states require that veterinarians keep up-to-date through continuing education, so Reggie attends lectures in veterinary specialties. Professional associations, such as the American Veterinary Medical Association, arrange these lectures.

Like physicians, veterinarians must have a *license* to practice. This ensures that they meet certain standards of practice determined by professional associations. To be licensed, veterinarians must pass various tests.

The Veterinarian of the Future

"There are lots of advances in veterinary medicine," says Reggie. "A lot of tests that in the past would be referred to specialists are now performed in hospitals." She believes that many veterinarians of the future will be specialists, such as cardiologists (heart experts). As for her own future, she is trying to decide if she wants to open her own hospital. It's a move that would require major financing and more administrative work than she has now. "I'm enjoying my present situation," she says.

George Timko

Chapter Two

WILDLIFE MANAGER

n March 1994, several species of seabirds began dying in the Chesapeake Bay area of Maryland. George Timko and a wildlife management team donned waders, rubber gloves, and rain suits and headed for the bay to pick up carcasses. Each day for several weeks, the team took dead and dying birds to the Maryland Center for Disease Control, where the disease was identified as avian cholera. Then the workers disinfected their equipment, right down to the vehicle tires. The cleanup was necessary to prevent uninfected birds from picking up the disease from sick or dead birds. Within three weeks, the team had stopped the disease. "We are here to conserve and protect," George says.

Fortunately, wildlife emergencies are the exception, not the rule. George works in a small wildlife station in western Maryland for the state's Fish, Heritage, and Wildlife Division.

George Timko

A Job That Changes with the Seasons

George's regular hours are 7:30 A.M. to 4:00 P.M., Monday through Friday, although he works weekends and evenings when he is needed.

Since wildlife management is a job that changes with the seasons, George's work is rarely the same. In spring and summer, he responds to calls from the public about nuisance animals, giving people advice about how to handle opossums, rats, and raccoons that are causing trouble. He also designs plans for wildlife habitats, prepares fields for replanting, and makes maps for private landowners who offer to grow crops to feed wildlife. "With man's destruction of the natural habitat," he says, "animals are finding it harder to fend for themselves."

In the fall and winter, George oversees managed hunting programs to control the population of game animals. He issues hunting and trapping licenses, provides information to hunters about hunting areas, and visits schools to talk to students about wild animals and their habitats.

George's fieldwork includes taking surveys to count the number of animals in a threatened species, such as a game bird called the woodcock. This lets scientists know how many of the animals are left in a certain area. The wildlife managers sit hidden in blinds (enclosures) to listen for the male bird's call and watch for the courtship ritual. When courtship brings the woodcocks into the open, the wildlife team can count the number of birds in the area.

On the Trail

George grew up in Baltimore. He lived near an abandoned military fort that had returned to its natural wild state. The quail, hawks, owls, and rabbits there aroused his interest in wildlife. After high school, he majored in wildlife and fisheries management at Frostburg State University. His courses ranged from biology and chemistry to report writing.

Upon graduation from college, George took his first job, as a trail technician, in one of Maryland's wildlife management areas. He planted gardens to feed wildlife and gave nature talks on the trail or in schools. Within

George works on a map showing areas where crops will be grown to feed wild animals.

George Timko

months, the wildlife division promoted George to natural resources technician, a job with greater emphasis on preserving wildlife habitats. He also fielded calls from the public about wildlife. He worked first at a wildlife station near Baltimore, then transferred to western Maryland.

George's career has followed a fairly typical path. "Fieldwork is where I want to be," he says. "But the more you advance to higher pay, the more administrative work there is." He is aiming for a happy medium between fieldwork and paperwork. He plans to study declining species and hopes to supervise field staff during population-counting surveys.

A Balancing Act

George must deal with difficult wildlife issues, such as how to control deer overpopulation. Some people favor controlled deer hunting, while others want to find different solutions, such as moving the deer to other areas. "People ask, 'Why are you killing Bambi?'" he says. "I try to keep things in perspective, to hear information on both sides of the debate and be scientific about it."

He notes that the deer's natural predators, such as wolves and mountain lions, are long gone. Many deer would compete for limited food supplies and starve to death without managed hunting. "It's in the best interests of the species," he says.

But George admits that he wasn't prepared for the hostility he's experienced from people who oppose hunting. "I don't like the negativity toward my career and what I do," he says. People sometimes forget the other side of his work—saving birds and animals injured by automobiles and returning healthy animals to wildlife areas.

What It Takes

A number of skills are important for a wildlife manager. George operates heavy farm equipment to plant crops for feeding wildlife. At the other extreme, he uses delicate surgical instruments during field necropsies (autopsies) on dead deer. These examinations help him gather information about the deer, such as how they died. Computer skills, spoken and written communication, and good health are also important for wildlife managers.

" Animals are finding it harder to fend for themselves. "

George likes fieldwork best, especially collecting scientific data. In order to get more field experience, he has volunteered to participate in several studies of Maryland's endangered species. One study in Maryland's Catoctin Mountains used 30 volunteers to fan out over rough terrain and count rattlesnakes. He also participated in other, smaller

George Timko

studies that counted and marked bog turtles and common map turtles. "I'd much rather spend time in the field," he says. "You're outside in the sun or in the rain and mud. It's hands-on."

But George also understands the need to write reports. "You need a written record," he says. Wildlife managers must analyze the information they collect to keep tabs on threatened species.

The Future

Wildlife management is a crowded field, with competition for jobs in all regions of the United States. Many of these jobs are for state or federal governments, and budgets are tight. George works as an hourly employee with no benefits like health care insurance or paid vacations. "I'm in it because I enjoy what I do," he says. "I'm getting the necessary experience."

George sees some changes in wildlife management careers of the future. "The antihunting sentiment is growing," he says. Because this pressure may cause a decrease in hunting, George believes that governments will collect less money from the sale of hunting licenses. Governments currently use the money from hunting licenses to pay wildlife managers, so future funding could be scarce. Most current wildlife managers work for government agencies such as the U.S. Department of the Interior. In the future, private organizations such as the Nature Conservancy, which seeks to protect wildlife by managing nature preserves, may hire more wildlife managers.

George's advice to those thinking about a career in wildlife management is to get some experience. But even volunteer work can be tough to find. He suggests that you become a wildlife observer for the U.S. Fish and Wildlife Service or the National Park Service, perhaps counting Canada geese or other migratory birds.

Other Careers in Wildlife Management

Most wildlife experts work for government agencies. The U.S. Department of the Interior and fish and wildlife agencies in every state employ wildlife managers. *Park rangers* oversee parks and monitor their use by the public. Many rangers conduct educational (interpretive) nature programs. *Animal control specialists* remove animals that create a nuisance around homes and other populated areas. *Game wardens* enforce laws protecting fish and wildlife.

Liza Herschel

Chapter Three

Zoo Educator

When Liza Herschel was young, she lifted up the large flat stones in front of her house to find out what was underneath them. That sort of curiosity stayed with her through college and several nature-related internships to her present job as education coordinator at the Baltimore Zoo in Maryland. "I'm always learning," she says. "I like to read and research."

Liza's job demands knowledge of animals and a friendly manner with people. She conducts classes and prepares written information for teachers who bring their students to the zoo. She also coordinates programs and events for zoo members, runs educational summer camps for children, and helps care for the small animals used in the zoo's educational programs.

Liza demonstrates the wingspan of a hawk, part of the Birds of Prey show she created for the Baltimore Zoo.

Liza also created a Birds of Prey show. It's been a hit with the public, particularly on summer weekends. Unlike many animal demonstrations, her show works with just two raptors, or birds of prey. During the show, she demonstrates a barn owl and a red-shouldered hawk, both with four-foot wingspans. "We do 20 minutes, flying them in front of groups. At the end, we take questions. People love it," she says.

During the summer when Liza presents the Birds of Prey show, she spends half her time working with animals. Her workday changes during the winter, when she researches, writes, and plans spring programs. "For example, we do a two-day African celebration. It's a collaboration with the Baltimore city schools. We include African wildlife," she says.

Orange Juice and Owls

Liza also has a few unusual responsibilities. The zoo's fund-raising staff sometimes asks her to bring animals to breakfasts hosted by the zoo to raise money. "It's orange juice and owls," she says. She also occasionally gets up before dawn to appear on early morning television shows with zoo animals. "I used to do theater. I thrive on attention," she says.

If this sounds like more than a full-time job, it usually is. The occasional seven-day workweeks can be difficult. "I wish I didn't have to put on summer camps," Liza says. She notes that another drawback of working for a zoo is the low pay.

Many nonprofit organizations rely on *fund-raising* to pay for their activities. Fund-raisers appeal to individuals and companies, often by hosting special events such as breakfasts, auctions, or parties.

Creating a Career Path

Liza has never confined her interests to one field. Although she did well in biology at Brown University, she majored in political science. In addition, she found a number of unusual opportunities. She taught a course in human sexuality to high school students,

worked as a counselor at a rape crisis center, and led a political science seminar for college students.

After Liza graduated, her teaching experience helped her land her first internship, at the Glen Helen Outdoor Education Center, a 2,000-acre animal preserve in Ohio. She received three weeks of training about plants, animals, and ecology and then taught a group of sixth graders. Since this was a residential program and her students lived at the center, Liza taught them for extended periods, sometimes all day. At Glen Helen, Liza had her first chance to study and work with raptors.

I created a career path without knowing it, following what I felt comfortable doing.

The following summer, Liza volunteered for a few weeks at the Wolf Fund, an organization reintroducing wolves to Yellowstone Park. By the fall, she was back interning at Glen Helen, this time as an outreach coordinator. She trained other naturalists and visited local schools to talk about animals' habits and habitats.

When this internship ended, Liza approached the Cincinnati Zoo. The zoo hired her as an unpaid interpretive (teaching) volunteer to conduct educational programs for visitors. "I talked to the public all day about Komodo dragons and walruses," she says. After three months, she began to earn an hourly wage. When a full-time job in the education division of the Baltimore Zoo opened up, her boss at the Cincinnati Zoo recommended her. "I created a career path without knowing it, following what I felt comfortable doing," Liza says.

The zoo's education staff consists of Liza, the director of education (who is her boss), a graphic artist, a volunteer coordinator, a technician who oversees care for the animals used in the education programs, two secretaries, a part-time coordinator of school programs, and two part-timers who clean and feed the animals.

New Zoos

Liza predicts the role of zoos will change and expand in the future. "Space in the wild is so reduced that zoos will become the last residences for many animals," she says. Zoos will also continue to educate people. The number of visitors has increased at new zoos that have open, natural habitats.

As for technology in zoo education, Liza mentions zoo programs on CD-ROMs and the use of e-mail to teach and answer questions from students. Both are part of the Baltimore Zoo's future. And although zoos may communicate with students in new ways, Liza believes that zoo employees will still need a flair for teaching.

"It's hard to get a zoo education job," says Liza. "You can't get into zoo education unless you prove yourself first." Internships, she

Other Zoo Careers

All zoos have a small army of people to keep things running smoothly. *Zookeepers* are on the front line, feeding the animals and cleaning cages. They watch for signs that an animal is sick or distressed. In some cases, they also train the animals and educate the public through shows. *Nutritionists* plan the animals' diets, and *animal behaviorists* work to develop the best way to care for the animals. The zoo's *veterinarians* monitor the animals' health. Zoos employ *zoologists* who specialize in mammals, birds, or reptiles. *Habitat designers* may work for the zoo or for companies that produce the natural-looking environments in new zoos. Other people work as *public relations experts, fund-raisers, groundskeepers,* or as part of the maintenance crew.

Professional and scientific jobs in zoos and aquariums are scarce. But jobs that require little education or that can be learned on the job—such as *groundskeeper* and *maintenance worker* positions—are sometimes open.

Zoos and aquariums also employ trainers who train animals, like this seal, for shows and demonstrations.

believes, are the answer. "It's the on-the-job training site." Liza suggests that students read environmental magazines for lists of internships. "Internships are plentiful, but you have to be willing not to make money," she says.

High school is not too early to get involved. Zoos all around the country have programs such as the Baltimore Zoo's Junior Keeper program. Each summer, 50 student volunteers (ages 14 to 18) are trained for five weeks to work on the zoo grounds and explain exhibits to the public. The second summer, volunteers may work in an animal department, such as birds or reptiles.

Liza is willing to let her future take her wherever it will. She lets herself dream a little: "I would love to be an expert on birds of prey and a world traveler." She laughs as she says, "I want to be Jim Fowler," the well-known television naturalist. Then she gets practical. Although she would jump at the chance to apply for the director of education job at the Baltimore Zoo, the reality is that her boss would have to move on to a different job first. "In zoos, it's hard to move up because everybody stays for a very long time," she says. "Most people have to go to another zoo to get the job they want."

David Harp

Chapter Four

WILDLIFE PHOTOGRAPHER

Wildlife photographer David Harp has a picture of himself when he was 12 years old. He is sitting in a boat, holding his first camera. "Now I do that all the time," he says, referring to his work photographing the Chesapeake Bay.

David works on wildlife and nature assignments for magazines such as *Smithsonian* and organizations such as the Nature Conservancy. He shot the photographs for two published books, a children's book about tundra swans, and a book for adults about the Chesapeake Bay. Although he takes corporate and advertising photographs to earn money, he spends about two-thirds of his time photographing nature and wildlife.

A Freelancer's Life

"For every day I photograph, I spend three in my office," says David. In his office/studio in a converted firehouse, he schedules photo shoots, researches wildlife habitats and habits, talks with clients about his photographs, handles the business details of billing and accounting, and prepares his marketing campaigns. "You have to get your name out to prospective clients," he says. "I do an enormous amount of writing—thank-you letters, proposals, invoices." File cabinets hold his slides in files by subject. A computer program keeps track of them.

As a freelance photographer, David works for himself rather than for a company or a boss. He provides service for a number of different clients. Because he must take care of his own accounting and record keeping, he says, "The business side of freelancing is the hardest part. I don't hate it, but it's not a lot of fun.

"There's no average day," he says. "When I'm shooting outside, I'm out long before sunrise. The best light is early in the morning. It's my special time. I also work in the evening." He may shoot in bad weather, since rain, sleet, or snow can often enhance the beauty of a photograph. And bad weather isn't the only difficulty. During a shoot for the Nature Conservancy, he took a wrong turn in the forest as night was falling. Eventually he came to a road, but he says, "I was tired and stressed and sweating and hot." Painful insect bites covered his body. It's not an

experience he cares to repeat. "But the pictures were beautiful," he says.

"Film is just light-sensitive plastic," says David. "You are judging the light and how to expose film, getting feelings on plastic. It's exhilarating." Also satisfying to him is the chance to show the public the harm that humans have done to the environment. "I don't think of photography as an art, but as a means of communication," he says. "I am showing somebody how I feel about something."

David sets up his camera in a river, where he hopes to see birds and wildlife. He may have to wait for hours before the right shot comes along.

Shooting Wildlife

"You need to be sensitive to animals," David says. "When you photograph a baby bird, you photograph it on its terms and not on yours. You don't stress it out." To photograph a great blue heron feeding its young, he spent 10 days building a blind. Then he waited another 10 days for the right moment to take a photo. After all the preparation, the photo took $\frac{1}{250}$th of a second to shoot. "You cannot go out in the woods and expect to get pictures. You do research, research, research. And more often than not, you come home with nothing."

Journalism Roots

David's photography career began when he was in high school. He took pictures for the small Maryland newspaper where his father was managing editor. Next David attended Ohio University, squeezing in courses in the earth sciences, journalism, and photography, in addition to his English major. After graduation, he returned to his hometown newspaper as a staff photographer. He was assigned to photograph news events, people, and places.

After David broke his leg in a skiing accident and was temporarily unable to drive, he left photography to promote tourism for his county. That led to a job with Maryland's Department of Tourism. There he wrote, designed, and produced brochures and audiovisual shows to encourage tourists to come to Maryland. *The Baltimore Sun* then hired him to do audiovisual shows for the newspaper. After six years, David grew tired of audiovisual work and resigned. A day later, the *Sun's* managing editor, who was familiar with David's work, invited him to become the staff photographer for the *Sunday Sun Magazine.*

" You need to be sensitive to animals. "

This was the job that focused David's career. He often found himself teamed with writer Tom Horton to produce nature articles. "I started learning and thinking and reading about nature and ecology and the environment," he recalls. Seven years later, he left the newspaper to freelance as a photographer.

Rapidly Changing Technology

Photography is entering a new age. Still-video cameras that take instant photographs will eventually replace traditional cameras, which require chemical processing of film. David already scans his photographs onto CD-ROMs for his clients to use. He has the equipment to transmit his images anywhere in the world with a modem.

In the future, David hopes to spend all his time photographing wildlife and nature. Since he grew up in Maryland, he specializes in photographs of the Chesapeake Bay region.

David Harp

Like many photographers, he sells the rights to use his photographs, but not the photographs themselves. That way he can sell the same images over and over to new clients. They are his "stock."

"My goal is to have fewer assignments of corporate work and more time to shoot stock photographs," David says. His plan mirrors a recent trend in which companies or publishers buy stock photos rather than assign photographers to a job.

Although the technology is changing, the basic skills of a wildlife photographer are not. "So much is learned by doing," he says. "To this day, I am learning. You get it by experimentation. You try to remember what worked and what didn't."

A nature photographer, David believes, needs to know more than photographic technique. "You need to learn about nature," he says. "If you understand it, your pictures have more depth." He mentions his photographs of the great blue herons. "I have photographed every stage of their lives" he says. His understanding of their life cycle helped him capture the best images.

David predicts that the already competitive world of photography will become overcrowded in the future. "You are never going to get rich," he says. Nature photography, he believes, is a lifestyle more than a job. "And I think you must have patience in your career and not expect things to happen all at once."

Learning Photography

You can major in photography at a fine arts school or study it as part of a college journalism major. Or you can attend a specialized college such as the Rochester Institute of Technology or a technical school in your community.

Most photographers begin taking pictures when they are young. They take photography courses in high school, at community centers, or at YMCAs. You can get photography experience on camping trips, in wildlife preserves, or at state or national parks.

David also recommends that you assist an established photographer, perhaps as early as your high school years. Although the pay may be low and the work sometimes tedious, the professional experience and business contacts that you gain are valuable. Photographers of the future, including nature photographers, will need to be computer-literate and business-minded.

Sandy Carrigan

Chapter Five

ANIMAL SHELTER SUPERVISOR

N othing surprises shelter supervisor Sandy Carrigan anymore. She has seen people adopt a puppy or a kitten, then bring it back when the pet was fully grown, because they didn't want it anymore. She has seen pets that have been run over by cars. She has seen dogs with gunshot wounds and cats mistreated by people who didn't know any better. Someone once left a dog tied to the gate of the shelter, which is run by the Maryland Society for the Prevention of Cruelty to Animals.

But Sandy has also seen dogs and cats recover from illnesses and terrible accidents. She has helped find homes for them with caring owners. She has seen lost pets reunited with their owners. "The best part of my job is seeing animals after they've been adopted," she says.

Sandy Carrigan

"Sometimes I get a letter or pictures. It really makes me feel good."

A Typical Day

Sandy, who is trained as a veterinary technician, spends each morning overseeing the care of the shelter's animals. She treats them for minor cuts, ear mites, or other ailments, and she conducts routine lab tests for parasites and viruses. In the afternoon, she creates the staff schedule and prepares an inventory (list) of controlled drugs in the shelter. The government requires the shelter to submit an inventory of prescription drugs. This ensures that only authorized people can use the drugs.

Sandy says hello to a dog in the kennel area of the sheler.

Then Sandy returns to check on the animals. "I like to spend time in the kennel area," she says, "talking to people and watching people." She has a good reason for this. The Maryland Society for the Prevention of Cruelty to Animals (SPCA) wants to make sure that people who adopt pets will take care of them. Over the years, by observing and talking to people, Sandy has developed a

" The best part of this job is seeing animals after they've been adopted. "

"sixth sense" about them. If she discovers during a conversation that someone does not have the space or money to care for an animal, she may deny the adoption. She must use firmness and tact. "You have to be a levelheaded and easygoing person," she says. "And you have to be compassionate."

Sandy's job is often rewarding, but it is also difficult. Although the SPCA encourages people to spay and neuter their pets to prevent unwanted puppies and kittens, many people do not. Each year, 40 percent of the animals that come to the shelter must be killed, because the shelter has no room for them. Euthanasia, or humanely killing animals, is a grim task and is the hardest part of Sandy's work. "It gets to you after a while," she says. But she knows that a pet abandoned by its owner may otherwise starve or die in a car accident. The shelter

does not have space for every abandoned animal.

A Lot of Responsibility

Sandy's job as a shelter supervisor is unusual. Unlike most other shelter supervisors, she lives on the Maryland SPCA's 11-acre estate. It's one of the benefits of the job. Her household includes two German shepherds, a Saint Bernard, a rottweiler, four cats, a talking parrot, a cockatiel, a canary, and an iguana. And those are just her own pets. Also under her care are the hundred or more animals living at the shelter at any given time. "I've always loved animals," she says.

After high school, Sandy studied psychology part time while she worked for a stable, helping transport horses to local racetracks. Next she worked as an office manager at a veterinary clinic. This job gave her on-the-job training and led to her enrollment in the veterinary technician program at Essex Community College.

Three years later, Sandy moved to another veterinary clinic as a vet technician. Here she assisted in surgery, treated sick animals, and helped with routine appointments. When the supervisor position at the Maryland SPCA opened up, her boss recommended her.

Sandy, second in command at the SPCA, keeps the shelter running smoothly day to day. She reports to the director, who is responsible for overall management and fund-raising for the shelter. Sandy supervises the office manager, the kennel attendants, the

**Sandy tests a urine
specimen in the lab.
Her job includes
routine lab work.**

receptionists, and the volunteers. She also
works closely with the education director,
who visits schools and talks to students
about pet care. A veterinarian comes in three
days a week to spay and neuter cats and dogs
to prevent overpopulation.

Sandy's job is a mix of paperwork and
hands-on work with animals. Although she
works from 8:00 A.M. to 5:00 P.M., since she
lives at the shelter, she often checks on the
animals on her days off. "But it's not like a
hospital, where the animals need attention all
the time," she says.

The Future

Since Sandy has
been with the SPCA for
less than a year, she is
not thinking too far into the

future. She's glad that her job offers health insurance, which many shelters cannot afford.

Sandy is concentrating on making improvements to the SPCA. Already she has changed the way the shelter keeps its medical records. She also began buying vaccines in bulk to save money. Since the Maryland SPCA is planning a major renovation, she has been visiting other shelters to get ideas for the new space. She would like to redesign the kennels to keep the animals more separated, to minimize the chance of spreading disease.

Sandy believes that people will always need animal shelters and professionals to work in them. "But it would be nice if the legislation was passed to require animals to be spayed or neutered before a pet could be purchased or given away," she says. "They do this in California."

What should you do if you want a career in a shelter? "Start out in a volunteer program," Sandy says. "Get hands-on experience. See if you like it." For instance, the Maryland SPCA uses teenage volunteers to walk dogs. "See if it's the field you should go into. You have to care about the animals. And you can't have any deep-rooted fears. Animals can sense it, even if you don't show fear."

She emphasizes that animal care is only part of her job. So, in addition to veterinary technician training, Sandy recommends that you take business administration and psychology courses in college to learn how to run a facility. "You get to deal with a lot of people," she says. "The people end of this job is what will make or break it for you."

Who Speaks for the Animals?

Some humane societies and animal shelters hire people to do promotional work to support the needs and rights of animals. Most of these careers do not require hands-on work with animals. *Educators* often visit local schools to teach children how to treat animals. *Writers* and *editors* prepare written materials— from brochures to lavish wildlife magazines—to inform the public about animals. *Lobbyists* for the Nature Conservancy, the Sierra Club, and other conservation groups try to persuade the U.S. Congress or local lawmakers to pass laws that benefit wild animals. *Animal rights activists* work for organizations such as People for the Ethical Treatment of Animals (PETA). Activists may demonstrate in costumes or picket research laboratories to bring the public's attention to animal rights.

David Secor

Chapter Six

FISH BIOLOGIST

Each spring and summer, fish biologist David Secor spends three to four weeks "out and about" on the Chesapeake Bay doing fieldwork. "I take samples of fish and monitor the water quality and temperature," he says. He also performs experiments to study the migrations of fish in the bay. Most of his treks into the field are day trips.

David's recent research at the University of Maryland's Chesapeake Biological Laboratory is aimed at determining the age of fish. "I can tell how fast fish are growing and dying and surviving year to year," he says. His purpose is to find out why fish populations have "crashed," or decreased suddenly. Recently, he proved that overfishing in the Chesapeake Bay during the 1970s resulted in 10 years of low numbers of fish.

David Secor

Teaching versus Research

David also teaches a course in fish biology at the University of Maryland. "But my main job is research," he says. His laboratory is on the lower Chesapeake Bay, but he teaches by interactive video so that students in other parts of the state can take his course. He finds teaching by video a little strange. "I'm like a weatherman," he says. "They see the side of my face."

David works from 7:00 A.M. to 5:00 P.M., but he rarely spends more than an hour or two a day in his research lab. "I miss it," he says. "Most scientists like laboratory work, but it's not productive to do full time." A lab technician and students under his supervision now do many of David's daily research chores. This arrangement gives David the time to write proposals that bring in money to pay for his research. For example, he recently designed a study to find out why fish migrated from one part of the bay to another. He then applied for a grant from the National Science Foundation to pay for the experiments. "You have to sell your ideas," he says. "The bad part is getting rejected, getting your proposal denied."

David also writes articles for scientific journals and books about his research. He spends part of his day reading other fish biology studies and making notes for his class. He also takes phone calls from people who want information about fishing in the Chesapeake Bay. Since he works on as many as five research projects at a time, he must schedule his workday carefully. "I make all

Research scientists test theories by collecting evidence and making observations. Scientists may do *fieldwork,* observing the subject in nature, or they may work in a laboratory, where they can make observations in a controlled environment. Many research projects involve a combination of fieldwork and lab work.

decisions. It can be stressful," he says. "If I don't do anything, nothing happens." He notes that self-reliance and creativity are vital to a researcher.

"The best part of the day," David says, "is when I learn something new. I can get pretty excited about it." What he likes a lot less is the record keeping.

" The best part of the day is when I learn something new. "

David also communicates with other scientists around the world through e-mail. "Collaborations are a big part of science. You can accomplish more working together than you can by yourself," he says. Two or three times a year, he attends conferences to exchange ideas with other researchers.

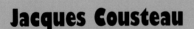

Jacques Cousteau

David grew up in Pennsylvania and Iowa. There were no oceans in sight, but marine explorer Jacques Cousteau's underwater adventures filled the television screen. "He left an impression of a different kind of world and how little we knew about it," David says. After high school, he studied biology at Macalester College in St. Paul, Minnesota. During a trip to the University of Hawaii, he met an aquaculturist, or fish

David Secor

farmer, who piqued his interest in aquaculture methods being used in Japan. After graduation from Macalester, David went to the University of South Carolina to study biology. He worked on his master's degree and learned Japanese. Then he headed to the University of Kagoshima in Japan for a year and a half as an exchange student.

"It was one of the most exciting times in my life," he says. "I even spent half a year in a remote fishing village learning aquaculture techniques." Although David fell in love with Japan, he found he didn't have the knack for

David spends a lot of time in and by the Chesapeake Bay.

aquaculture. "It's like gardening—you either have a green thumb or you don't. I didn't have a 'blue thumb.'" He decided instead to return to the University of South Carolina to get a doctoral degree in biology.

David's first job was as a "post-doc" researcher, or post-doctoral fellow, paid by a research contract at the University of Maryland's Chesapeake Biological Laboratory. This full-time job lasted three years. When a permanent research and teaching position opened, the university chose David over 80 other candidates because of the importance of his research for the future of fish in the Chesapeake Bay.

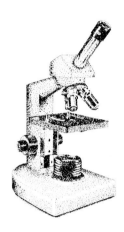

The Future of Marine Biology

David thinks the future of marine biology will be a combination of applied science—scientific knowledge that is used in a practical way such as fish farming—and pure research. "Any progress in science is good. But it's very important to make human connections," he says. David's research is the first step in increasing the supply of fish for people to eat.

Marine biology is the study of the plant and animal life in the ocean or sea.

Although the field of marine biology is becoming more "applied" and practical, what makes a good scientist remains the same. "The creative skills can't be overemphasized," David says, referring to a researcher's talent for dreaming up new ways to discover scientific information. A scientist, David believes, needs to work alone *and* build a support network of other scientists. Because

The Animal Sciences

Many science careers involve animals. These careers require years of advanced education, usually a Ph.D, or doctorate, which is the highest academic degree. Competition for full-time positions with good salaries, benefits, and job security is intense. Most biologists work for universities, government agencies such as the U.S. Department of the Interior, zoos, aquariums, private corporations such as biotechnology firms, and nonprofit organizations such as the Sierra Club.

Animal scientists often specialize. *Zoologists* are biologists who study animals, not plants. *Mammalogists* study mammals. *Entomologists* learn about insects and *herpetologists* about reptiles and amphibians. *Ornithologists* study birds. *Paleozoologists* study ancient animals and fossils and *ecologists* examine organisms in their environment.

A researcher observes baboons in Africa.

marine biology is a crowded field, you need persistence and motivation to find work.

David advises that you study math, biology, and chemistry and get research experience in high school and college through internships and summer programs. "You must enjoy the day-to-day stuff. Learn early if you like research," he says.

As for his own future, David thinks in terms of questions, not jobs. "I'm interested in 'big picture' kinds of questions. Why do fish move? How do they use their habitat? Why do some fish survive and others not?" he says. "It will take a whole career to answer these questions."

A biologist measures the temperature of hibernating bats in a cave in Indiana. Many jobs in science involve animals.

Debbie Winkler

Chapter Seven

ANIMAL BEHAVIORIST

I have a fundamental understanding of how to make a dog or a cat do something," says animal behaviorist Debbie Winkler. She makes use of a dog's instincts and abilities to encourage certain behaviors. "I create a working environment that allows dogs to do what they naturally want to do," she says. Early in her career, Debbie worked with a dog trainer who used less humane methods. "I learned what I didn't want to do with my dogs," she says. "I was uncomfortable with the animals cowering."

Debbie trains signal dogs, sometimes called "hearing ear" dogs, for hearing-impaired people. Dog Ears, Ltd., is her nonprofit company. Donations pay for the training, which can take 10 to 20 months.

Dog Ears, Ltd.

Like many freelancers or self-employed people, Debbie works long hours. She also trains ordinary companion dogs and teaches dog obedience classes at a local kennel in the evenings and on weekends.

Debbie Winkler

Debbie's mornings begin with the administrative work necessary to keep Dog Ears running. She takes calls from hearing-impaired clients, who use a Telephone Device for the Deaf (TDD) that displays written messages. She answers questions from her private clients, writes letters, pays bills, and calls charitable organizations to ask for contributions. Her deepest frustration is finding enough money to keep Dog Ears in business. "It's always a struggle," she says.

Debbie visits a client at her home. She trained the dog to be a companion to the woman, who has multiple schlerosis.

Debbie devotes certain days or afternoons to Dog Ears' clients. Debbie or her volunteers, some of whom are high school or university students, often follow up with home visits to work with both dogs and owners. That's because signal dogs need refresher courses to help them remember their training or to solve problems that arise.

For example, a signal dog is trained to nudge its owner when a telephone or doorbell rings and then move toward the sound. But the dog has to learn a different response to a smoke alarm: not to go toward the sound. Instead, Debbie teaches the dog to lie flat on the floor in front of its owner as a signal. Because smoke alarms rarely go off, the dog must practice this behavior occasionally.

An Unregulated Field

"I was always interested in animals and in people and what motivates them to do things," says Debbie. As a child, she remembers encountering people with disabilities. "I was told, 'Don't look or stare.'" She made a point of talking to them. "The response was overwhelming," she says. "They told me, 'People avoid me and people don't look at me.'" The experience left a deep impression.

After high school, Debbie worked for a veterinarian, feeding the animals and cleaning up, while she went to college part time. She earned a degree in behavioral sciences at George Washington University and took psychology and sign language

Debbie Winkler

courses at other colleges. Dog training, she notes, is a field with no educational requirements. On-the-job training counts more than formal education.

Debbie's job with the veterinarian also gave her insights. "I learned how animals behave under stress," she says. When she worked for an animal hospital in her teens, she learned to "read" animals and people, she says.

I create a working environment that allows dogs to do what they naturally want to do.

When Debbie began a job with another veterinarian, she planned to learn animal grooming. But then she began working with a dog trainer, who became her mentor, or teacher. "It was the beginning of something wonderful in my life," she says. She stayed for five years at the kennel and then formed Dog Ears, Ltd.

Repetition and Practice

"Dog training is a lot of repetition," says Debbie. "It's very monotonous, like practicing a musical instrument." Not everyone has the right temperament for dog training.

She especially enjoys teaching disabled people how to interact with their animals so the animals can help them lead more independent lives. Dog trainers know that they are not just training dogs—they are also training owners to give their animals the proper commands. "I am serving people," Debbie says. "They have more confidence and are more independent. This is what motivates me."

Debbie has plans for the future. Since the demand for signal dogs is so great, she hopes to teach others to train signal dogs. She is

Debbie visits a dog that she trained.

Dog Training

Seeing eye or guide dogs get their training at 12 independent centers around the United States. You can contact the National Federation of the Blind to find the location closest to you (see page 109). Mobility-assist dogs—dogs trained to help the elderly and people in wheelchairs—are often trained by volunteers in nonprofit organizations. Veterinarians or animal organizations often can supply information.

Law enforcement officers also use trained dogs in their work. Dogs track missing persons or sniff out drugs, bombs, or plants brought into the United States illegally. Local police units, airports, private security firms, and government agencies (such as the FBI and the U.S. Department of Agriculture) use trained dogs. Private organizations, individuals, or trainers working for these law enforcement agencies train the dogs.

Many police departments use trained dogs.

studying a program in a California women's prison in which inmates are taught to train signal dogs. She recently approached the governor of Maryland to develop a similar program in her state.

Debbie has some advice for people who hope to train dogs: "Volunteer for humane societies or get a part-time job for a vet," she says. "Or forget the animal end of it and volunteer to feed people in a nursing home. You need to see the whole picture, animal and human." She notes that a dog trainer who works with disabled people needs natural optimism. "You have to be up. Some situations are tragic. You need infinite patience," she says, "and you have to have compassion for living creatures. There is no room to be critical and judgmental. You need to accept people the way they are."

A Labrador retriever acts as a guide dog for his master, who is blind.

Steve Wilson

Chapter Eight

DAIRY FARMER

Steve Wilson's 250-acre dairy farm lies in the rolling Maryland countryside. From a distance, the white buildings and the black and white Holstein cows create a traditional picture. But behind the scenes, computers, high-tech gadgets, and modern agricultural methods run the show.

Around the neck of each cow, for example, hangs a computer chip that activates the animal's grain feeder. Steve can control the amount and the timing of the cow's feeding with this technology. He notes that nutrition relates directly to his "bottom line," or profit.

Steve understands the usefulness of technology, but he also knows its limits. "You eyeball a lot," he says. He knows that if the cows' feet are red, their feed has too much acid. If their hair is brown, the feed has too much copper. "You must have the confidence to challenge the computer," he says. "It comes from experience." He also just happens to know the name of each of his animals.

Steve Wilson

The Longest Day

Steve's day begins about 4:00 A.M., when he gets up for the first milking. At 7:30 or 8:00, he has breakfast, then feeds the calves. In addition to Steve's milking and feeding chores, his job includes five hours a week of office work. He pays bills, reviews soil tests that tell him how nutritious his crops are, and orders feed and equipment. He works in either his barn or his home office. Both are equipped with computers. The second round of milking and calf feeding begins at about 4:00 P.M. Steve's day often ends after 7:00 P.M. "There is no day when I get up and have no responsibilities," he says.

Since farming is seasonal, the time of year largely determines Steve's work between milkings. In the spring, he fertilizes his fields and plants alfalfa, corn, and hay. "We make hay every 30 to 35 days after about May 10th. But July and August are surprisingly slow," he says. He uses the summer months to repair his equipment or buildings. September and October are busier, since three or four calves are born every day. He gets little sleep in the fall and often wakes up in the middle of the night to check on a sick cow. "I don't need much sleep, but if I'm really tired, I'll grab a 10-minute nap at lunch," he says.

By the middle of November, Steve's work slows. One day a week, he attends gatherings of farmers, feed merchants, and agricultural extension agents. These agents work for the local university or the U.S. Department of Agriculture and introduce farmers to the latest agricultural research. The meetings

Steve's daily chores include feeding and milking the cows.

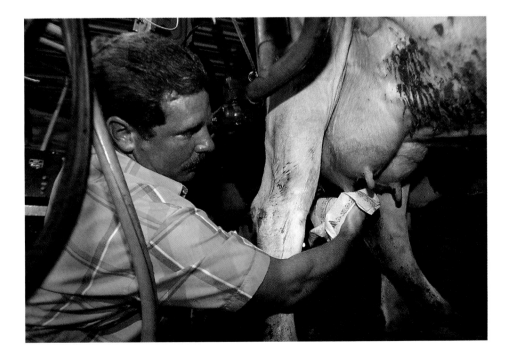

Steve Wilson

allow him to keep up with new farming methods. In addition, he subscribes to many agricultural newsletters and magazines, such as *The Dairyman* and *Small Farm Today.*

The Family Farm

Because this is Steve's family's farm, he grew up working here after school, in the summer, and on weekends. "It was drudgery until I was 16 or 17," he says. Then he became interested in cattle breeding, herd health, and nutrition. After high school, he studied agriculture for a year at the University of Maryland before he took over the day-to-day farm management from his father.

Steve can't run the farm alone. At any given time, he needs two to five farmhands. Many specialists—veterinarians, nutritionists, and the brokers who sell feed—also help him. Like many farmers, Steve fixes his own equipment and breeds livestock to keep costs down and save time. "I don't take as much time off as I should," he says. What does he do in an emergency? Steve relies on neighboring farmers to help. "If someone has a problem, once the word is out, all of them come and help out. It's what makes farming such a great thing," he says.

A family farm

New Technologies

Keeping up with the newest technologies is important to all farmers. Steve needs to use these new methods, not just for the health of his herd, but for the health of his bank account as well. Steve keeps an open mind about scientific discoveries, including the results of biotechnology research. This research has created changes in the basic genes of plants and animals to produce hardier species. "It's scary and it's very interesting," he says. He recently tried a new drug to boost milk production. But he

"You must have the confidence to challenge the computer. It comes from experience."

stopped using the drug when he found that the cost of the drug was more than the money he earned from the extra milk. Steve must also watch his herd carefully for side effects from new drugs.

Future Farmers

Steve is not optimistic about the future for small farmers. Family farms, he says, particularly those in the mid-Atlantic region of the United States, are finding that making a profit is harder and harder all the time. He predicts that most U.S. farms in the future will be large and located in the Midwest. Large companies that hire farm managers to oversee daily operations already control many farms. If his own farm becomes

Other Agricultural Careers

Dairy farming and cattle ranching are becoming more computerized and businesslike, just as all agricultural careers are. Large corporations will hire farm managers to manage the daily operations and work with up-to-the-minute technologies to raise food animals.

Many future agricultural careers will be scientific. *Agricultural researchers* will look for better ways to eliminate farm pests and diseases and develop hardy animal species through biotechnology and genetics. Informing farmers about new technologies will continue to be the work of government or university *agricultural extension agents. Computer experts* will help farm managers with day-to-day business tasks on the farm, such as accounting and record keeping. *Environmental scientists* will discover ways to keep the soil from being overused.

unprofitable, Steve will manage a farm for someone else.

In a job with few vacations and little free time, what keeps him going? "I love what I do," he says simply. He enjoys living in tune with the seasons and loves helping a cow deliver a calf. "It's literally a matter of life and death," he says. What frustrates and tires him is the constant concern about making a profit.

Careers in farming are wide open—on and off the farm—both for highly educated workers and those with little education. "Finding good people is hard," Steve says. He and other small farmers are willing to train young people, even those with no experience in farming. They are always looking for responsible workers who want to learn farming. As with so many other jobs working with animals, practical experience in farming—feeding livestock, planting and harvesting crops—counts most. Steve believes that most people are not aware that modern equipment and methods have changed the hard physical work involved in farming. "I work less hard physically than I ever have," he says. "What keeps people away from farming are the hours. And the responsibility. There are good days and bad days."

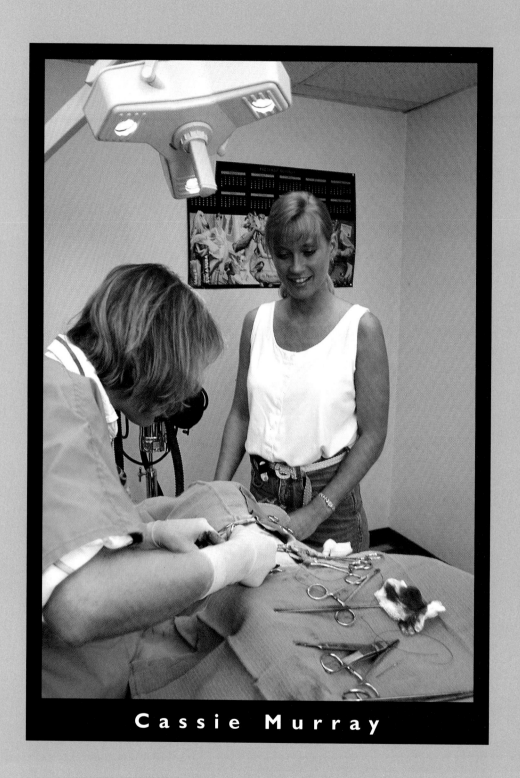

Cassie Murray

Chapter Nine

VETERINARY TECHNICIAN

People worry more about their pets than themselves," says Cassie Murray. "Clients are wonderful when they have puppies. But they are as tough as they can possibly be if they have a sick pet." After working as a registered veterinary technician in an animal hospital for 10 years, Cassie has learned to identify with their worries. "I have to remember how I felt when my pet had surgery or was sick," she says. "Then I can relate to their five phone calls in five hours. Communication skills are the number one thing."

A Fast-Paced Day

Cassie works six days a week, from 8:00 A.M. until 2:00 P.M., except Tuesdays, when she stays late. She doesn't work any nights, because the hospital refers clients to an emergency animal clinic. "This

Cassie Murray

place is fast-paced," she says, referring to the steady stream of cats and dogs that come in for their annual visits. "You don't eat lunch or you eat on the run." Since Cassie has diabetes and requires regular doses of insulin, her schedule was troublesome until she began using an insulin pump to keep her blood sugar level steady. "If you need a regimented lifestyle, this is definitely not a good field," she says.

Cassie's days begin with rounds of the hospitalized pets. She checks cuts and stitches and gives medications. Then office hours and appointments start. "I talk with clients, take pets' weights and temperatures, and find out what the animals are here for. I get any vaccines ready," she says. She notes problems, such as fleas or ear infections, on the animal's chart. She may also help restrain or calm an animal. She has been nipped several times. "Usually my reflexes are good enough to get away," she says.

Cassie devotes her afternoons to assisting the veterinarian with surgery. "I will hold a dog to anesthetize it, although I don't administer anesthesia. I prep dogs for surgery, shave the site, and get surgical instruments ready."

The first few times Cassie helped with surgery were frightening. "I walked into the treatment room and saw a dog flat on its back with its legs tied out. It was a shocking scene," she says. Then there's always the chance that the pet might react badly to the anesthesia. Although the risk of dying is slight during routine surgery, some animals do die. "That's heartbreaking. You remember that," she says.

Anesthesia, used on animals and humans during surgery, prevents the patient from feeling pain.

Cassie also has to help the veterinarian euthanize old and suffering pets. "The first time was during my clinical internship. It was an Irish setter. I held the animal. I cried for days and I dreamed about it for weeks. I still cry in the room when we do it," she says. "But euthanasia is not painful. It's an overdose of anesthesia. The animals lie down and go to sleep." This task remains the hardest part of her job.

A Tough Program

Cassie grew up wanting to be a veterinarian. But she could not afford the seven or eight years of college and veterinary school. The veterinary technician

Cassie assists the vet during surgery. The dog is under anesthetic, with a breathing tube in its mouth.

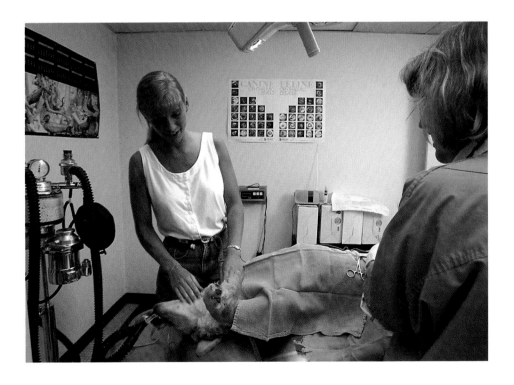

Vet Tech Programs

There are veterinary technician programs nationwide, in all but a few states. Admission requirements vary, but most schools require high school science and math courses, a high school diploma, references, and an interview. Many vet tech programs recommend that students do volunteer work at an animal hospital before applying to school. Programs can take two to three years to complete.

Every state has its own requirements and tests to become registered, licensed, or certified as a veterinary technician. Some states, however, have no requirements or tests. The national exam is a written test. State tests vary, but all of the tests examine basic vet tech skills in surgery and animal care.

Most registered veterinary technicians work in hospitals treating pets, mostly dogs and cats. Other technicians are employed by veterinarians who work with large animals (such as horses and cattle), on farms or at universities, research laboratories, zoos, and aquariums. Duties vary according to the setting and the types of animals.

program at Essex Community College offered another choice. In addition to biology, anatomy, chemistry, and microbiology, she took practical courses in laboratory and surgical procedures, animal diseases, and nutrition. "The program was much tougher than I expected," she says.

Cassie's program also required two clinical internships in veterinary hospitals. "I lucked out," she says. "They were short staffed, so I got paid. Most people don't." Although she earned only minimum wage, she also earned college credit for the work. Upon graduation, Cassie passed the written national exam and the practical Maryland state exam to become a registered veterinary technician. She spent the next couple of years as a veterinary technician at another hospital, but now she is back at the hospital where she interned.

The advantages of college training and state registration over on-the-job training are higher pay, better choice of jobs, and more responsibility. Although veterinary assistants who train on the job can, by law, do what Cassie does, many veterinarians prefer to work with registered technicians.

Cassie also sees registered technicians as important to the future of veterinary medicine. "People are looking for quick and inexpensive pet care. Veterinary technicians are less expensive to pay."

She predicts that future "vet techs" will take on some of the routine tasks that veterinarians now perform. She expects that animal hospitals will be larger and will hire more registered veterinary technicians.

Cassie Murray

Best Therapy in the World

"I like working with the animals. They are the best therapy in the world," says Cassie. "I'm a much happier person when I'm around young, healthy pets and happy people." Even when the work is draining, she goes home fulfilled. She didn't always feel this way, though. When she was promoted to office manager, she did only billing and scheduling. That lasted six months. "At the end of the day, there was no physical feeling of accomplishment," she recalls. "I need to deal with the pets," she says. Now Cassie does both. "It's given me more variety and better pay."

Vet tech salaries are low—sometimes not much better than minimum wage. Most

Cassie does billing and scheduling on the computer. She likes to have a mix of office work and hands-on work with animals.

Managerial work is not fulfilling for me. I need to deal with the pets.

animal hospitals do not provide health or vacation benefits. As a result, some registered technicians go back to school to become veterinarians, pharmacists, or nurses. Cassie may eventually change careers, too. On the upside, she says, "The work is different every day. It's not a boring job."

Cassie's career recently took a new turn. The faculty at Essex Community College invited her to teach the introductory course in the veterinary technician program. Teaching is a new challenge, one that may offer new opportunities.

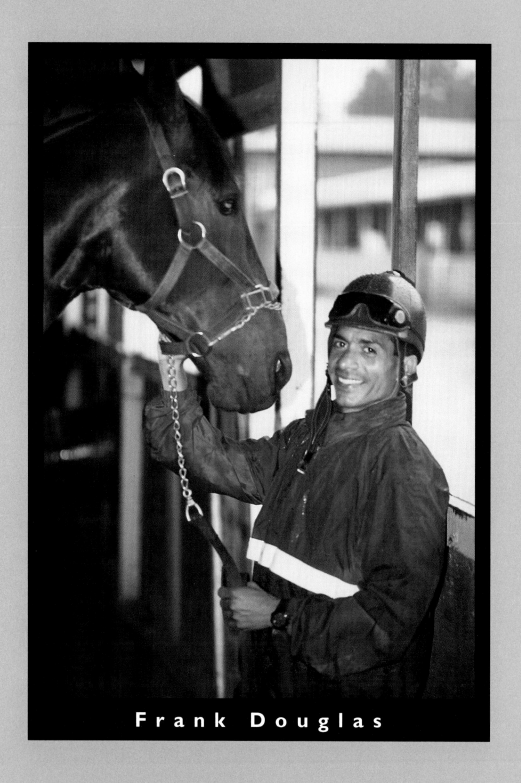

Frank Douglas

Chapter Ten

JOCKEY

Racing horses for a living, says jockey Frank Douglas, has a lot in common with show business. "It's like trying to get a part in a movie. You are the actor. And you go to the trainer, who is like the director." Not surprisingly, Frank grew up with horses and loves racing. "You have to love it to do it. You have to have it in your blood."

Frank believes a horse race is a mental activity as much as a physical one. "You have to think. The whole idea is to make the horse win or to get the best out of the horse," he says. "You have to look to see where you are going. You have to keep out of trouble." Every horse has a burst of energy during the race. The job of the jockey, Frank says, is to think about when to use that burst of energy to win the race.

A Different World

Frank's day begins about 5:30 A.M. Since he is self-employed, each morning he visits his clients, trainers who hire him to ride their horses in races at Maryland racetracks. Frank discusses with the trainer how best to work with each horse.

Frank Douglas

Then he may also ride a little. "You have to be out there every day," he says. Some trainers have many horses, owned by different people. If you refuse to ride one horse, Frank says, they may not hire you to ride others. He flashes a quick smile. "I try not to use the word 'no.'"

In the afternoon, Frank gets ready for his races. Each racetrack has a jockeys' room with a kitchen, recreational facilities, and a

Frank changes out of his racing clothes in the jockeys' room.

place to sleep. "I like to come early to get mentally ready," Frank says. He rests and concentrates on the races ahead. Then he dresses in the traditional "silks," or jockey uniform. Each owner, Frank explains, has special colors that the jockey wears. The racetrack employs a "color man" to care for the jockeys' silks.

"Sometimes you ride afternoons and evenings," says Frank. "It's exhausting but good for business." He may ride in 20 or 30 races a week. Maryland racetracks are open year-round, but some tracks in other parts of the United States have a much more limited season. In that case, jockeys must move from state to state to find work.

Jockey School

Racing *is* in Frank's blood. He was born in Panama, where his grandfather was a horse trainer. After attending a military high school, Frank studied business administration in college for a couple of years, first in Panama and later in Washington, D.C., where his father was a diplomat. Then Frank returned to Panama to attend a school for jockeys. There he learned horse care, exercise riding, and racing techniques.

Unlike Panama, the United States has no schools for jockeys. Instead, American jockeys train on the job. "An American jockey has to find a trainer to teach him all about the horse business and trust him on his horses," Frank says. Most jockeys begin as hot walkers, groomers, or exercise riders at a racetrack.

After graduation, Frank returned to the United States. He worked first at a racetrack in West Virginia, then at one in Philadelphia. During this time, he was an apprentice jockey. Although apprentices ride in regular races, they usually become professional only after five wins and at least one year of experience. Jockeys must be licensed by the states in which they race. Frank has licenses to race in Maryland, New Jersey, West Virginia, Pennsylvania, and Delaware.

The Future of Racing

The racing industry is changing, Frank says. Legal betting parlors can show live telecasts, called simulcasts, of races from any track, local or out of state. People can bet on the races without going to the track. This increases the money a track makes. But the televised races may make it harder for jockeys to earn a living, because some tracks may close.

Jockeys have joined together to form the Jockeys' Guild, a professional association that protects their best interests.

Frank remains hopeful about the horse racing tradition. He believes that faster horses and faster tracks have made the sport exciting. For those who love riding, being a jockey won't change.

Frank isn't definite about his own future. "I'll do this as long as I can," he says. He notes that in racing, as in many sports, athletes may lose their ability to compete at a top level as they grow older. Most jockeys retire in their early 40s. When he does retire from racing, Frank plans to become a trainer, a jockey's agent, or a horse owner.

Jockeys must watch their weight carefully—they have to stay slim.

Frank Douglas

What It Takes

Being a jockey is dangerous. When Frank broke his arm in a fall in 1989, he couldn't ride for four months. "But I don't have fear. If you've got fear, you better quit riding," he says. Then he laughs as he looks down at a broken ankle. He broke it playing softball. "If it's going to happen, it's going to happen. It's life. I've come to terms with it," he says. But injuries *can* be bad for a career. "With injuries, you lose your clients and you lose horses for the time being," he says.

" You have to have racing in your blood. "

A jockey has to maintain a low weight. "I only eat in the afternoons," Frank says. "Other times I have vitamins and coffee." Although most nutritionists would be unhappy with that diet, Frank's weight has remained between 110 and 112 pounds, about average for a jockey. Most jockeys are between 5 feet 2 inches and 5 feet 4 inches tall.

A jockey needs a will to win, combined with a happy nature and an even temper, Frank says. "If you have a bad attitude, you don't get the horses. You can't be angry or you can't show it. You can't get a reputation as a troublemaker. I have to be a businessman, a public relations person, an ambassador," he says.

Other Jobs Working with Horses

Most racing employees learn on the job. People who own horses hire *trainers* to supervise the care of their horses. Trainers often have horses from several owners in their stable. The trainers hire jockeys, *exercise riders* to gallop their horses each morning, *groomers* to care for the horses and stalls, and *hot walkers* to walk the sweaty horses after each race. Jockeys, in turn, hire *valets* to care for their saddles and harnesses. Many jockeys hire *agents* to find clients (owners and trainers) in return for a percentage of the jockey's earnings. Not all jockeys have agents.

Horse farms and riding stables also have jobs for those interested in working with horses. They employ trainers, groomers, exercise riders, and *riding instructors.* Like many jobs at the racetrack, pay at farms and stables is low, the hours are long, and the outdoor working conditions can be tough. On-the-job training is standard for careers with horse farms and stables.

Barbara Littleton

Chapter Eleven

PET SITTER

Every pet sitter has a tale or two to tell. Barbara Littleton's favorite story stars Howie, a bullmastiff and Great Dane mix, and a German Shepherd named Max. During one visit, Barbara stepped outside to get the owner's mail, accidentally leaving the house key on the table near the door. She quickly realized the key wasn't in her hand. It was too late. "Howie and Max jumped up and closed the door and locked me out," she says, laughing. "I had to get a locksmith."

Although Barbara has had few pet-sitting emergencies, she admits that one icy winter was difficult. But because she interviews new clients at length, she had prepared herself with emergency phone numbers and names of family members, friends, and neighbors. On days when the roads were too icy for her to drive, she arranged for clients' neighbors to feed the pets.

Barbara Littleton

Long Hours and Satisfaction

As the owner of PetWatch, a pet-sitting service, Barbara tries to meet the needs of animals and owners. "I fit into the routine the pets are accustomed to. I try to make them feel comfortable," she says. "The owners can go away and know that everything is okay at home."

Pet sitters work long hours and weekends. Barbara's clients often pay her to visit their pets in their homes three times a day, from early morning to late at night. "Sometimes I stay longer than an hour. It depends on my rapport with the animals and how much they want attention," she says. In addition to

feeding, walking, and playing with the animals, she waters plants, takes in mail, and checks the house. For some clients, she will stay overnight.

As for working seven days a week, Barbara admits the schedule bothers her sometimes. And the financial rewards aren't great. Not surprisingly, summer and Christmas are her busiest times. "The money varies so much. It's the downside of pet sitting, unless you have regular dogs to walk."

A Career Path with Detours

Dogs, cats, opossums, fish, birds, frogs, and caterpillars populated Barbara's childhood home in Baltimore. She remembers feeding a neighbor's cat when she was a child. "It's always been a casual gesture," she says. "People don't think of

"People are funny about their pets."

pet sitting as a business. But it's more commonplace now."

Barbara has known for a long time that "people are funny about their pets." She has one client, for example, whose dog is 18 years old and eats cereal for breakfast and bean soup for dinner.

Barbara's first job after graduating from high school was working for a veterinarian. She learned to assist at surgeries, to draw

Barbara Littleton

blood, to clean teeth and ears, and to insert the needles that allow medicine to flow into an animal's veins. "I tell new PetWatch clients my own history," she says. She knows that her veterinary experience makes clients comfortable with leaving their pets in her care.

After four years, Barbara left her veterinary assistant job to join the U.S. Coast Guard. She trained and worked as a cook. Three years later, during military budget cutting, she took an "early out" and returned to Maryland and got a job as a cook in a local detention center.

PetWatch

The desire to work with animals was again on Barbara's mind. When she read an article in the magazine *Entrepreneur* about a woman who ran a pet-sitting service, Barbara sent for the woman's book. Then she and a friend established PetWatch.

They needed to plan and develop the business, but they did not need much start-up money. "We stuffed flyers in people's mailboxes, put them in stores, and at all the veterinary hospitals," she says. They bought advertising in local newspapers and noted which ads brought in customers. Telephone directory advertisements still generate three or four calls a week.

During PetWatch's early years, Barbara's partner took care of the finances and the daily dog walks for their regular clients. "I took care of the phone calls and new client interviews and the people on vacation," Barbara says. The PetWatch owners arranged for insurance to protect themselves and their clients from financial loss if something happened when PetWatch was on the job.

Then Barbara's partner left PetWatch when her full-time job became too demanding. Barbara has not yet found another partner or hired employees. She says this is partly because her regular clients expect her, not a substitute, to care for their pets. Because she works alone, she has reduced the paperwork. Clients leave their payments for her in their homes or mail her a check. Although this arrangement would make many business owners anxious, for PetWatch, it works fine.

Because money from PetWatch is uncertain, Barbara works as a pet sitter only part time. She left her cooking job at the detention center, so she helps support herself by working part time for a cleaning service. Barbara's immediate goal is to go back to work for a veterinarian. Her long-range plan is to run PetWatch full time. She also dreams of helping others start pet-sitting services, perhaps even selling PetWatch franchises, or branches of her business that would be owned and run by other people. "I've had calls. People say, 'Show me how you got started.' But I don't know how this would work," she says. "I need to find people who take ideas and put them into motion." She plans in the future to talk to marketing, finance, and legal experts to find out more about selling PetWatch franchises.

Doggy Day Care

Barbara believes pet sitting has a big future. Many people

Other Pet Service Jobs

Pet services are big business. *Breeders, kennel owners* and *managers, pet groomers,* and *pet store owners* all provide services for pets. Larger kennels may hire *attendants.* Many people who provide pet services are self-employed and learn on the job. Pet groomers sometimes learn their trade through vocational schools. The pay for pet service careers depends on experience and skills. New pet superstores also offer opportunities, but the work is mostly clerical or managerial, with little actual contact with animals.

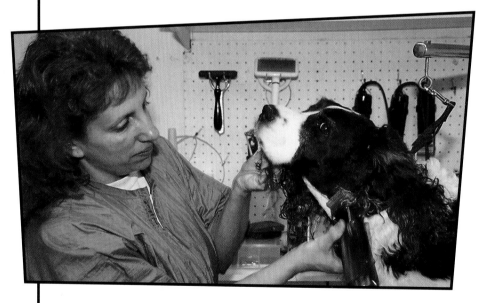

Some pet groomers work in their homes and others set up their business in an office.

work long hours and need to rely on others for pet care. Although the nature of pet sitting will not change, she thinks people may specialize by offering services, such as taking a pet to the veterinarian. In Germany, she says, dogs can spend the day at a day care center while their owners are at work. Day care centers for pets may spring up in the United States.

Barbara suggests that future pet sitters work first as a volunteer or a paid assistant in an animal hospital. Local veterinarians sometimes hire older teens. Or they can care for friends' and neighbors' pets, as she once did. "Get some confidence," she says. "You need rapport with animals *and* pet owners." She also believes that strong communication skills and certain personality traits are essential. Pet sitters need self-reliance, a willingness to work long hours, and flexibility. "You have to have a certain rapport. It's a natural thing, not an acquired skill," she says. Pet sitters, she notes, also have to feel comfortable going into people's homes and finding their way around strange neighborhoods at night.

M i k e   B u r d e t t e

Chapter Twelve

AQUACULTURIST

Set among green pastures dotted with ponds, and surrounded by tall trees, the Burdette farm has been in the family for generations. Wild Canada geese touch down on a pond that is stocked for sportfishing. But the ponds are no longer where the action is. To see the cutting edge of fish farming technology that is replacing the commercial fishing boats of the past, you have to go into a garagelike building. Aquaculturist Mike Burdette gestures toward a large room of fish tanks. "My father calls this Edison's Lab," he says, referring to inventor Thomas Edison. On the far side of the room, a computer monitors oxygen levels and temperatures in the tanks.

Mike manages Maryland Pride Farms, a commercial fish farm, with some part-time help from his brother Brian. Their father, Doug Burdette, designed their successful aquaculture operation—a system of fish tanks and water recycling equipment controlled by computer software. "It's like a dream," says Mike, "to see something we started in a place the size of a four-car garage. And we've built it into one of the best systems in the world."

Mike Burdette

A Working Farm

"One person could run the farm, but he would work seven days a week," Mike says. His workday begins about 8:00 A.M. It takes him two or three hours to "clean down" the water filtration system, check the filters, rinse the tanks, and clean the oxygen probes so they will not give false readings. The water is filtered so that wastes are piped away and clean water returns to the fish tanks. The whole process is monitored by computer.

Mike checks on the oxygen level in the fish tanks.

Next Mike feeds the fish (they eat high-protein grain pellets) and observes them to make sure they are eating. "After you do it for a month, you know how the fish respond," he says. He also stays within hearing range of the alarm. "We've developed a system that goes off *before* there is an actual crisis," he says. Slight temperature changes or low oxygen levels in the tanks could trigger the alarm.

Mike spends the rest of his day developing new aquaculture equipment. "I like research and development. I can use my imagination," he says. He adds, "I could live without cleaning out the fish tanks." Mike also manages some fishing tournaments on the family's ponds.

"This is not an office job. But you can make an honest and good living at it," he says. He predicts good prospects for decent pay and plenty of career opportunities in the future. "It's a good career, but don't limit yourself to hands-on work," he says. Other careers exist in research, helping others set up fish farms, or marketing new varieties of fish to the public.

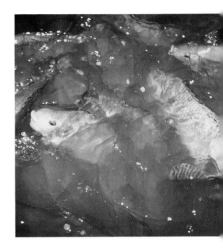

The American Dream

The story of how the Burdettes started fish farming is the story of the American dream. In the late 1970s, when Mike's father, Doug Burdette, was driving a tractor trailer, he noticed that other truckers delivered two loads of catfish from Texas to Baltimore each week. He decided a local fish farm could make a good profit. "We started digging ponds," says Mike. They raised rockfish, catfish, and talapia, a Middle Eastern fish new to the United States. Local fish markets that sell to Chinese restaurants buy as much fish as the Burdette farm can supply. The Burdette farm, which has been recognized for its creative methods of aquaculture, will soon have 32 tanks.

Mike credits his family with having many of the skills needed to build a fish farm. His grandfather owned a septic tank business and knew a lot about wastewater systems. His uncle, his father, and Mike all had experience in construction, welding, and working with fiberglass, which gave them the skills to build a tank system. Mike is also a diesel mechanic, trained to repair the big rigs his father used to drive. After six months of technical school, Mike worked for three years at two tractor-trailer dealerships while working at the fish farm part time. In 1989 he became a full-time aquaculturist.

Fast-Growing Aquaculture

Aquaculture is the fastest growing segment of American agriculture. Overfishing and pollution of the oceans, rivers, and lakes have ravaged natural fish populations. "By the year 2000, I see aquaculture as mandatory," Mike says, foreseeing a time when there will be no significant harvest of fish from the ocean. "Our seafood has got to come from aquaculture."

Maryland Pride Farms already can't keep up with the demand for their fish. Every week they sell over 300 pounds to Baltimore markets. As they add more fish tanks, they expect to ship as many as 10,000 pounds of fish each week to markets throughout the East Coast. The largest fish farms produce up to 50,000 pounds a week. Because the Burdettes also do research and development work, they do not raise as many fish as other farms do.

Mike and his father predict a future in

which they will sell not just their fish but aquaculture franchises. "If we can get a system rolling and out on the market, it'll be a franchise no different than McDonald's," he says. They plan to provide computer hookups, aquaculture training, and technical support over the phone to people who buy the franchises. Already the Burdettes study proposals for prospective fish farmers to help them make good investments. And they sometimes provide software and build tank systems for new fish farms.

Mike describes how they test their systems to find out what works best: "We try to do every stupid thing that could go wrong and see what the computer does." For example, even though the filters that recycle water need daily cleaning, he has purposely neglected the filters to see how the system would react. "It's not a pretty picture," he

Our seafood has got to come from aquaculture.

admits with a laugh. "And the economics are bad. The oxygen bill will go up and the fish may not have the right taste."

Not by chance does he mention economics. The Burdettes' computer tracks oxygen rates in the fish tanks—and it also tracks profits. The tank system allows them to grow two pounds of fish per gallon of water, which is twice the industry average. In

Mike Burdette

addition, their system uses the fish wastes from the recycled water as fertilizer to grow crops in a greenhouse on the farm. Sales of plants can increase profits.

A Promising Future

The technology of aquaculture is changing fast, and the future looks promising. Colleges offer aquaculture courses and may soon offer aquaculture majors. The Burdettes think the academic programs have their place, but both Mike and Doug believe that nothing takes the place of practical skills learned from the daily

At a commercial fishing pond, fish are raised to be sold.

The Future of Commercial Fishing

The commercial fishing industry is in trouble. By 1992, 40 percent of the world's natural fishing grounds were overfished. By the 21st century, making a living by fishing the seas—from Maine to the Pacific Northwest—may well be a thing of the past.

care of fish tanks and greenhouses. Mike also suggests that you learn about computers. He believes that the knowledge gained from accounting, marketing, and business courses is more important to successful aquaculture than the study of biology. "You really only need biology if you are getting into genetics, creating special breeds of fish." He also makes a confession: "I'm the type who doesn't pick up a lot from reading, but show me a picture and I can build what I see." He is working on an aquaculture invention that he hopes to patent in the future.

Indoor fish farms are scattered all over the United States and Canada, occasionally even in the middle of cities. Mike's advice for future aquaculturists? "Visit a fish farm. See what you are in for. Don't be afraid to ask questions," he says. "Open your mind to things."

To Continue Exploring...

Veterinary Medicine

American Veterinary Medical Association
1931 North Meacham Road, Suite 100
Schaumburg, IL 60173-4360
(708) 925-8070

North American Veterinary
 Technicians Association
P.O. Box 224
Battle Ground, IN 47920
(317) 742-2216

Wildlife Management

National Parks and Conservation Association
(also publishes *National Parks* magazine)
1776 Massachusetts Avenue N.W., Suite 200
Washington, DC 20036
(202) 223-6722

National Wildlife Federation
1400 16th Street N.W.
Washington, DC 20036-2266
(202) 797-6800

The Nature Conservancy
1815 North Lynn Street
Arlington, VA 22209
(703) 841-5300

Sierra Club
730 Polk Street
San Francisco, CA 94109
(415) 776-2211

U.S. Fish and Wildlife Service
U.S. Department of the Interior
Washington, DC 20240

Wildlife Management Institute
1101 14th Street N.W., Suite 801
Washington, DC 20005
(202) 371-1808

The Wildlife Society
5410 Grosvenor Lane
Bethesda, MD 20814-2197
(301) 897-9770

National Wildlife
(National Wildlife Federation publication)
8925 Leesburg Pike
Vienna, VA 22184-0001
(703) 790-4524

Sierra
(Sierra Club publication)
730 Polk Street
San Francisco, CA 94109-7813
(415) 923-5653

Zoos and Aquariums

American Association of Zoo Keepers
Topeka Zoological Park
635 S.W. Gage Boulevard
Topeka, KS 66606-2066
(913) 272-5821

American Association of Zoological Parks
 and Aquariums
Oglebay Park, Route 88
Wheeling, WV 26003
(304) 242-2160

American Society of Zoologists
401 North Michigan Avenue
Chicago, IL 60611-4267
(312) 527-6697

Zoo Life magazine
Ingle Company
11661 San Vicente Boulevard, Suite 402
Los Angeles, CA 90049
(310) 820-8841

Wildlife Photography

American Society of Media Photographers
14 Washington Road, Suite 502
Princeton Junction, NJ 08550-1033
(609) 799-8300

Professional Photographers of America
57 Forsyth Street N.W., Suite 1600
Atlanta, GA 30303
(404) 522-8600

Animal Shelters

*Check your local telephone directory for
shelters near you.*

American Society for the Prevention of
 Cruelty to Animals (ASPCA)
424 E. 92nd Street
New York, NY 10128
(212) 876-7700

The Humane Society of the United States
2100 L Street N.W.
Washington, DC 20037
(202) 452-1100

People for the Ethical Treatment of Animals
P.O. Box 42516
Washington, DC 20015
(301) 770-7444

Marine Biology

American Institute of Biological Sciences
730 11th Street N.W.
Washington, DC 20001-4521
(202) 628-1500

CEDAM International
(association of marine biologists)
1 Fox Road
Croton Hudson, NY 10520
(914) 271-5365

Center for Marine Conservation
1725 DeSales Street N.W., Suite 500
Washington, DC 20036
(202) 429-5609

Marine Technology Society
1828 L Street N.W., Suite 906
Washington, DC 20036
(202) 775-5966

* *Dolphin Log* magazine
The Cousteau Society
870 Greenbrier Circle, Suite 402
Chesapeake, VA 23320-2641
(804) 523-9335

Animal Behavior

American Dog Trainers Network
161 W. Fourth Street
New York, NY 10014
(212) 727-7257

Assistance Dogs of America
8806 State Route 64
Swanton, OH 43558
(419) 825-3622

Guide Dogs for the Blind
P.O. Box 151200
San Rafael, CA 94915-1200
(415) 499-4000

National Federation of the Blind
1800 Johnson Street
Baltimore, MD 21230
(410) 659-9314

Farming and Ranching

* National 4-H Council
7100 Connecticut Avenue
Chevy Chase, MD 20815-4999
(301) 961-2820

* National FFA Organization
  (also publishes *FFA New Horizons*)
5632 Mount Vernon Memorial Highway
Box 15160
Alexandria, VA 22309-0160
(703) 360-3600

Horse Racing

Jockeys' Guild
250 W. Main Street, Suite 1820
Lexington, KY 40507
(606) 259-3211

Pet Sitting

National Association of Professional
  Pet Sitters
1200 G Street N.W., Suite 760
Washington, DC 20005-4709
(202) 393-3317

Groom & Board magazine
H.H. Backer Associates, Inc.
20 East Jackson Boulevard, Suite 200
Chicago, IL 60604-2383
(312) 663-4040

Pet Business Magazine
5400 N.W. 84th Avenue
Miami, FL 33166-3333
(305) 592-9890

Aquaculture

World Aquaculture Society
143 J.M. Parker Coliseum
Louisiana State University
Baton Rouge, LA 70803
(504) 388-3137

General Detective Work

* *American Careers* magazine
Career Communications, Inc.
6701 W. 64th Street
Overland Park, KS 66202
(913) 362-7788

* specifically for kids

INDEX

ABOUT THE AUTHOR

Barbara Lee is the author of *Death in Still Waters: A Chesapeake Bay Mystery*, which won St. Martin's Press' 1994 Best First Malice Domestic Mystery Novel Contest. A New Yorker, she now lives in Maryland.

ACKNOWLEDGMENTS

The photographs and illustrations in this book are reproduced courtesy of: Churchill Downs, Inc., p. 88; © Kent and Donna Dannen, pp. 27, 67, 80; Lee Engfer, p. 97; Darren Erickson, p. 57; Andy King, pp. 6, 8, 10, 11, 12, 14, 16, 18, 20, 23, 25, 28, 30, 32, 36, 39, 41, 44, 46, 47, 49, 51, 52, 55, 56, 60, 63, 64, 65, 68, 71, 73, 76, 79, 82, 83, 84, 86, 89, 90, 100, 102, 103, 105; Maine Office of Tourism, p. 34; Minneapolis Public Library and Information Center, pp. 33, 35, 42; Bill Munoz, pp. 87, 91; Ontario Ministry of Agriculture, Food, and Rural Affairs, p. 72; Red Rock Lakes National Wildlife Refuge, p. 24; Dan Rosenberg/Alaska State Parks, p. 26; USDA Photo, p. 74; Mario Villafuerte, pp. 2, 92, 94, 95, 96; Visuals Unlimited, p. 43 (Arthur Morris), p. 58 (C.P. Hickman), p. 59 (Richard Thom), p. 66 (W.A. Banaszewski), p. 98 (Jeff Greenberg), p. 106 (A.J. Cunningham); Wisconsin Department of Natural Resources, p. 22.